Also by Jaroslaw Jankowski

Why Are We So Different?
Your Guide to the 16 Personality Types

Why are we so very different from one another? Why do we organise our lives in such disparate ways? Why are our modes of assimilating information so varied? Why are our approaches to decision-making so diverse? Why are our forms of relaxing and 'recharging our batteries' so dissimilar?

Your Guide to the 16 Personality Types will help you to understand both yourselves and other people better. It will aid you not only in avoiding any number of traps, but also in making the most of your personal potential, as well as in taking the right decisions about your education and career and in building healthy relationships with others. The book contains the ID16$^{TM©}$ Personality Test, which will enable you to determine your own personality type. It also offers a comprehensive description of each of the sixteen types.

The Animator

Your Guide
to the ESTP Personality Type

The ID16^{TM©} *Personality Types series*

JAROSLAW JANKOWSKI
M.Ed., EMBA

This is a book which can help you exploit your potential more fully, build healthy relationships with other people and make the right decisions about your education and career. However, it should not be considered to be a substitute for expert physiological or psychiatric consultation. Neither the author nor the publisher accept any responsibility whatsoever for any detrimental effects which may result from the inappropriate use of this book.

ID16™© is an independent typology developed by Polish educator and manager Jaroslaw Jankowski and grounded in Carl Gustav Jung's theory. It should not be confused with the personality typologies and tests proposed by other authors or offered by other institutions.

Original title: Twój typ osobowości: Animator (ESTP)
Translated from the Polish by Caryl Swift
Proof reading: Lacrosse | experts in translation
Layout editing by Zbigniew Szalbot

Published by LOGOS MEDIA

Paperback: ISBN 978-83-7981-054-3
EPUB: ISBN 978-83-7981-055-0
MOBI: ISBN 978-83-7981-056-7

Contents

Preface

The work in your hands is a compendium of knowledge on the *animator*. It forms part of the *ID16*TM© *Personality Types* series, which consists of sixteen books on the individual personality types and *Who Are You? The ID16*TM© *Personality Test*, an introduction to the ID16TM© independent personality typology, which is based on the theory developed by Carl Gustav Jung.

As you explore this book on the *animator*, you will find the answer to a number of crucial questions:

- How do *animators* think and what do they feel? How do they make decisions? How do they solve problems? What makes them anxious? What do they fear? What irritates them?

- Which personality types are they happy to encounter on their road through life and which ones do they avoid? What kind of friends, life partners and parents do they make? How do others perceive them?
- What are their vocational predispositions? What sort of work environment allows them to function most effectively? Which careers best suit their personality type?
- What are their strengths and what do they need to work on? How can they make the most of their potential and avoid pitfalls?
- Which famous people correspond to the *animator*'s profile?

The book also contains the most essential information about the ID16$^{TM©}$ typology.

We sincerely hope that it will help you in coming to know yourself and others better.

ID16™© and Jungian Personality Typology

ID16™© numbers among what are referred to as Jungian personality typologies, which draw on the theories developed by Carl Gustav Jung (1875-19161), a Swiss psychiatrist and psychologist and a pioneer of the 'depth psychology' approach.

On the basis of many years of research and observation, Jung came to the conclusion that the differences in people's attitudes and preferences are far from random. He developed a concept which is highly familiar to us today: the division of people into extroverts and introverts. In addition, he distinguished four personality functions, which form two opposing pairs: sensing-intuition and thinking-feeling. He also established that one function is dominant in each pair. He became convinced that each and every person's dominant functions are fixed and independent of external conditions and that, together, what they form is a personality type.

In 1938, two American psychiatrists, Horace Gray and Joseph Wheelwright, created the first personality test based on Jung's theories. It was designed to make it possible to determine the dominant functions within the three dimensions described by Jung, namely, **extraversion-introversion**, **sensing-intuition** and **thinking-feeling**. That first test became the inspiration for other researchers. In 1942, again in America, Isabel Briggs Myers and Katherine Briggs began using their own personality test, broadening Gray's and Wheelwright's classic, three-dimensional model to include a fourth: **judging-perceiving**. The majority of subsequent personality typologies and tests drawing on Jung's theories also take that fourth dimension into account. They include the American typology published by David W. Keirsey in 1978 and the personality test developed in the nineteen seventies by Aušra Augustinavičiūtė, a Lithuanian psychologist. Over the following decades, other European researchers followed in their footsteps, creating more four-dimensional personality typologies and tests for use in personal coaching and career counselling.

ID16^{TM©} figures among that group. An independent typology developed by Polish educator and manager Jaroslaw Jankowski, it was published in the first decade of the twenty-first century. ID16^{TM©} is based on Carl Jung's classic theory and, like other contemporary Jungian typologies, it follows a four-dimensional path, terming those dimensions the **four natural inclinations**. These inclinations are dichotomous in nature and the picture they provide gives us information regarding a person's personality type. Analysis of the first inclination is intended to determine the dominant **source of life energy**, this being either the exterior or the interior world. Analysis of the second inclination defines the dominant **mode of assimilating information**, which occurs via the senses or via intuition. Analysis of the third inclination supplies a description of the **decision-making mode**, where either mind or heart is dominant, while analysis of the fourth inclination produces a definition of the dominant **lifestyle** as either organised or spontaneous. The combination of all these natural inclinations results in **sixteen possible personality types**.

One remarkable feature of the ID16™© typology is its practical dimension. It describes the individual personality types in action – at work, in daily life and in interpersonal relations. It neither concentrates on the internal dynamics of personality nor does it undertake any theoretical attempts at explaining or commenting on invisible, interior processes. The focus is turned more toward the ways in which a given personality type manifests itself externally and how it affects the surrounding world. This emphasis on the social aspect of personality places ID16™© somewhat closer to the previously mentioned typology developed by Aušra Augustinavičiūtė.

Each of the ID16™© personality types is the result of a given person's natural inclinations.

There is nothing evaluative or judgemental about ascribing a person to a given type, though. No particular personality type is 'better' or 'worse' than any other. Each type is quite simply different and each has its own potential strengths and weaknesses. ID16™© makes it possible to identify and describe those differences. It helps us to understand ourselves and discover our place in the world.

Familiarity with our personality profile enables us to make full use of our potential and work on the areas which might cause us trouble. It is an invaluable aid in everyday life, in solving problems, in building healthy relationships with other people and in making decisions relating to our education and careers.

Determining personality is a process which is neither arbitrary nor mechanical in nature. As the 'owner and user' of our personality, each and every one of us is fully capable of defining which type we belong to. The individual's role is thus pivotal. This self-identification can be achieved either by analysing the descriptions of the ID16™© personality types and steadily narrowing down the fields of choice or by taking the short cut provided by the ID16™© Personality Test.[1] The role played by each 'personality user' is equally crucial when it comes to the test, given that the outcome depends entirely on the answers they provide.

---

[1] The test can be found in *Why Are We So Different? Your Guide to the 16 Personality Types* by Jaroslaw Jankowski.

Identifying personality types helps us to know both ourselves and others. Nonetheless, it should not be treated as some kind of future-determining oracle. No personality type can ever justify our weaknesses or poor interpersonal relationships. It might, however, help us to understand their causes!

ID16™© treats personality type not as a static, genetic, pre-determined condition, but as a product of innate and acquired characteristics. As such, it is a concept which neither diminishes free will nor engages in pigeonholing people. What it does is open up new perspectives for us, encouraging us to work on ourselves and indicating the areas where that work is most needed.

The Animator (ESTP)

THE ID16™© PERSONALITY TYPOLOGY

The Personality in a Nutshell

Life motto: Let's DO something!

In brief, *animators* ...

are energetic, active and enterprising. Fond of the company of others, they have the ability to enjoy the moment and are spontaneous, flexible and open to change.

Animators are inspirers and instigators, spurring others to act. Being logical, rational and pragmatic realists, they are wearied by abstract concepts and solutions for the future. Their focus is on solving concrete problems in the here and now. They have difficulties with organising and planning and can be impulsive, acting first and thinking later.

The *animator's* four natural inclinations:

- source of life energy: the exterior world
- mode of assimilating information: via the senses
- decision-making mode: the mind
- lifestyle: spontaneous

Similar personality types:

- the Administrator
- the Practitioner
- the Inspector

Statistical data:

- *animators* constitute between six and ten per cent of the global community
- men predominate among *animators* (60 per cent)
- Australia is an example of a nation corresponding to the *animator's* profile[2]

The Four-Letter Code

In terms of Jungian personality typology, the universal four-letter code for the *animator* is ESTP.

---

[2] What this means is not that all the residents of Australia fall within this personality type, but that Australian society as a whole possesses a great many of the character traits typical of the *animator*.

General character traits

Animators are active and spontaneous. They focus on today and have the ability to enjoy the moment, preferring to make the most of what life offers them here and now, rather than being the kind of person who spends much of their time wondering what the future will bring. With their liking for variability and the unexpected, they will readily get involved in anything new that comes their way.

Animators have difficulty staying in one place and continually hunger for new impressions and experiences. Once they have delved into a field of knowledge and found the answers to a question that has been nagging them or acquired new skills, they are off again, spotting new challenges and problems to be solved. As a rule, they have no difficulty in adapting to new circumstances and find changes easy to handle. In fact, they look forward to them!

Perception

In general, *animators* are pragmatists and realists, relying on what can be touched, seen and heard. Splendid observers and outstanding in their perceptiveness, they distrust presentiment and intuition. *Animators* learn by practical action, finding theoretical arguments and abstract concepts wearisome. Open by nature, they are tolerant and understanding both of others and of themselves. They have the ability to forgive themselves a great deal and are not given to torturing themselves with recollections of past mistakes or poor choices.

Decisions

When *animators* make decisions, they are guided by logic. Rational arguments and evidence speak louder to them than their personal feelings and intuition. Their decisions are usually reactions to situations and needs which have emerged and more rarely the result of conscious and planned preparation for something they anticipate in the future. They will often 'think out loud'; discussing problems with other people and putting various possibilities into words helps them to arrive at a solution.

When they decide to act, they pay little attention to how people around them will respond to what they do. First and foremost, they follow their own convictions, which are grounded in rational and objective facts. Faith in their own principles is not only more important to them than satisfying other people, but even takes precedence over observing prevailing norms and customs.

As others see them

Other people see *animators* as compassionate, spontaneous and open. In general, they are considered to be energetic, active, practical and extremely direct; indeed, some people find them too direct. They are often viewed not only as very welcome company when it comes to having a good time, but also as people whose help can be relied on when problems suddenly crop up. Much more rarely will they be perceived as experts in tasks demanding good planning and sensible organisation; in fact, they sometimes have a reputation for being disorganised, if not chaotic. Those who are devoted to the unselfish service of others or focused on the life of the spirit often take *animators* to be superficial people with their interest fixed on building a career and material things.

In turn, *animators* have trouble understanding those who are fascinated by abstract theories or concepts. Fans of sentimental novels, melodramas and soap operas are also a source of bewilderment to them.

Problem solving

Being practical by nature, *animators* have no liking for lengthy digressions on the theme of what should be done, but would rather just roll up their sleeves and get straight on with things. They prefer practical, concrete tasks and will often subconsciously monitor their surroundings, seeking out problems that require solving. On the whole, they need little time to prepare, being always 'on their marks, set and ready to go'. They excel at coping in circumstances demanding fast reactions, flexibility and improvisation. While others are overcome by emotion or paralysed by fear in emergency situations – such as search and rescue actions, for instance – *animators* keep their heads and stay cool, evaluating the situation rapidly and objectively and taking whatever action is vital. In addition, their reactions keep pace with changing circumstances and new factors and they have the ability to shift the thrust of their activities and adapt them to fresh conditions in a flash.

They cope less well with tasks which demand planning and lengthy preparation. In situations of that kind, they will try and save the day by means of that superb talent for improvisation which is so typical of the *animator*. Nonetheless, it can happen that, as a result of their problems with planning and their rather deficient organisation of their work, they end up losing out on all sorts of opportunities and failing to make the most of myriad 'chances of a lifetime'.

Animators are prone to overestimating what they can manage; for instance, they might underrate the amount of work necessary to accomplish a task. They will thus sometimes leave too much until the last minute, putting their colleagues and their nearest and dearest through a host of stressful experiences. Planning and organisation may not be numbered among their strengths, but even so, with a little effort, they are capable of developing those skills to a considerable extent.

Communication

Animators dislike expressing their thoughts in writing and much prefer the spoken word. They have a colourful turn of phrase and the gift of persuasiveness. Being more ready to speak than to listen, they are usually impatient. As such, they might well interrupt the people they are in conversation with, without letting them finish. However, their openness, optimism and sense of humour make other people happy to listen to them. All of this, in conjunction with their active nature and enthusiasm, means that, where an *animator* goes, others will follow. They are often the instigators and animators of all kinds of activities ... hence the name for this personality type.

When they set out on a new venture, they have the ability both to infuse others with faith in its success and to encourage them to act. However, by nature, they are better at initiating an activity than seeing it through to the end. They have more problems than most with keeping their promises and sticking to previous arrangements; when a new challenge appears on the horizon, their enthusiasm for the things they have already started doing will simply vanish. This attitude will sometimes cause disappointment to those who, encouraged by their initial commitment, joined them in an activity they initiated.

In the face of stress

Animators are capable of working well and are just as good at relaxing. They have the ability to 'switch off' and give themselves over completely to unwinding or having fun without feeling the slightest pang of conscience on that account. They will often have a particular love of sport and active leisure pursuits. As a rule, they cope well with stress in situations of conflict. If the tension drags on, though, it can lead to their exhaustion, loss of energy and withdrawal. When wearied and fatigued, they may seek powerful sensory experiences, turning to substances or looking for thrills in gambling or risky financial speculations.

Socially

Animators are open to people, which makes them approachable and easy to get to know. They will usually win the liking of those around them and are able to fit in with a new 'crowd' and adapt to whatever situation they find themselves in. They are known for the way they can regale people for hours with amusing stories and for their ability to come out with witty comments on reality. Their very presence alone will often be enough to take the strain out of a tense atmosphere. Remarkably direct in their dealings with others and prone, in general, to speaking their mind, they can also be impulsive and explicit. Indeed, their critical remarks might be hurtful to people who are more sensitive and emotional.

Being impervious to criticism and pressure from those around them, *animators* are unlikely to waste time on inquiring about what others think of them and how they perceive them. They are capable of influencing people and even of manipulating them in order to achieve goals they consider to be important.

Although they brighten things up for the people who spend time with them and are often the life and soul of the party, they frequently have problems with deeper interpersonal relationships. If they are forced to enter the world of emotions and feelings, their 'inner compass' fails them and, in no time at all, they are hopelessly lost. As a rule, they find it easier to forge bonds when the focal point is having fun or tackling problems together; developing relationships rooted in feelings comes much harder to them. As a result, family relations can pose a greater challenge to them than professional ones.

Amongst friends

Where's the action? Wherever it is, that is where *animators* will want to be. They like the company of others, love having fun with them and are always up for any kind of 'team' venture, as well as being quick to adapt and feel at home with new people, and in new surroundings and circumstances. Others appreciate their enthusiasm, optimism and sense of humour and will happily spend time with them. They are usually seen as gregarious, spontaneous and uncomplicated.

Animators like striking up acquaintanceships. Happy to get to know new people, the focus of their friendship shifts more often than in others. After a brief conversation, they will already have sized up the potential of people they have only just met. The problems start when it comes to reading their emotions and feelings. Their spontaneity and impulsiveness mean that other people quite often take them to be emotional. In reality, though, they are guided first and foremost by logic and common sense.

When it comes to spending time with others, variety is most certainly the spice of an *animator's* life. Spontaneous and quick to make decisions, they would definitely rather see everyone up and doing something together; in the long run, sitting around a table and chatting bores them to tears. *Animators* are a prime example of people who prefer deeds to words and their family and friends know that, if a practical problem needs a fast solution, they can always count on their help. Practical action is their way of expressing their friendship and affection. They most often make friends with *administrators*, *practitioners*, *innovators* and other *animators* and, most rarely, with *mentors*, *counsellors* and *idealists*.

As life partners

Animators are dynamic, energetic and sensual, with a spontaneity and sense of humour which make it impossible to be bored in their company. As a partner, they bring vitality and energy to the relationship; life will never be dull with an *animator* around. In general, they set great store by freedom and find restrictions hard to endure. By the same token, they impose no restraints on their partners, but give them free rein.

Animators care deeply about their partner's needs and are highly supportive. However, actions speak louder than words in their case and it is practical needs, rather than emotional, which carry more weight with them, since they themselves have few of the latter and thus have difficulty perceiving them in their nearest and dearest. As a rule, they also have trouble with reading and showing feelings, though with a modicum of effort, they are able to develop those skills over time. The nature of their romantic disposition can mean that their partner feels hurt by the lack of compliments, affection and endearments and might also suffer on account of the *animator's* critical remarks and unkind jokes.

In general, *animators* will have no truck with talking about feelings and relationships, finding discussions of that kind not also tiresome but also a waste of time that would be better spent doing something concrete. To a sensitive and emotional partner, the *animator's* conversations with them might appear shallow and superficial, while their responses can give the impression of being rather too terse.

A powerful new stimulus will normally rivet the *animator's* attention so firmly that, as they become absorbed in the latest challenge, their previous undertakings may well fly right out of their minds. Once an insoluble problem or unexplored puzzle intrigues them, there is very little that can stop them from becoming engrossed in it and, as a result, they often have trouble with keeping previous promises. This will sometimes evoke a sense of frustration in their partner, particular when they do not share the *animator's* enthusiasm or have no understanding of the essence of whatever is currently absorbing them.

Animators live for the moment, which is why the vow "to have and to hold (...) till death do us part" might represent a considerable challenge to them. Their nature is to view undertakings of that kind as decisions which are made anew on a daily basis. Life with an *animator* may be a constant adventure, thanks to their spontaneity and love of change, but those same characteristics can sometimes be a threat to the stability of their relationships. Their perpetual fascination with new acquaintances and their inclination to flirt are also potential hazards.

The natural candidates for an *animator's* life partner are people of a personality type akin to their own: *administrators*, *practitioners* or *inspectors*. Building mutual understanding and harmonious relations will be easier in a union of that kind. Nonetheless, experience has taught us that people are also capable of creating happy and successful relationships despite what would seem to be an evident typological incompatibility. Moreover, the differences between two partners can lend added dynamics to a relationship and engender personal development. Indeed, for many people, this is a prospect that appears more attractive than the vision of a harmonious relationship wherein concord and full, mutual understanding hold sway.

As parents

The *animator* parent treats their children as independent people, asking for their viewpoints, counting on their opinions and being ready to admit that they are right and even to learn from them. They encourage their offspring to explore the world and make active use of their free time. Partnership parenting is their preferred style and they are more like friends than mentors, searching for the answers to questions and discovering the world together with their children.

Rather than adopting the role of experts proffering ready answers to just about anything, they are not embarrassed to admit to not knowing something. In general, they are tolerant, uncomplicated and understanding, though they can sometimes be impulsive and impatient and their efforts at raising their children are often lacking in cohesion and inconsistent. If the other parent is unable to operate in a more organised fashion, their children might lack a sense of security and stability, as well as clear rules establishing how the world is run.

Animators often have problems with disciplining their offspring, a duty which they are only too happy to cede to their partner. On the other hand, they love playing and having carefree fun with them, deriving just as much joy from it as the children. Indeed, they will sometimes be so involved that all thought of their other responsibilities vanishes from their minds. By the same token, though, when they are engrossed in some other activity, it is their children who are well-nigh forgotten.

It can sometimes be difficult for children to understand their *animator* parent and their switchback tendency to focus entirely on playing with them some of the time and be utterly inaccessible on other occasions. Another cause of problems in parent-child relationships is the difficulty *animators* have with reading and expressing feelings. They are not, by nature, the kind of parents who shower their children with endearments and wrap them in warmth on a daily basis. Their natural mode for showing their love is their solicitude for their offspring's needs, particularly in the practical sphere, a responsibility they take extremely seriously. When their child is facing some kind of trouble, they are capable of swinging straight into action, doing whatever is necessary without delay. For instance, if they hear of any problems occurring in their children's school, they will not only be the first to intervene, but will also spur other parents to act as well.

Once adults, their children are grateful to their *animator* parent for allowing them so much freedom, encouraging them to explore the world and getting them out of trouble when things got difficult. They will also have fond recollections of all the crazy fun they had together.

Work and career paths

Wherever the action is, that is where *animators*, with their love of variety, will be happy to work. They fit in well in organisations which value activeness and enterprise and give their employees a free hand in accomplishing their tasks, but handle strict supervision and constantly being checked up on very badly and dislike immovable deadlines, rigid structures and bureaucratic procedures. When they are convinced they are in the right, they are capable of consciously ignoring the relevant instructions or regulations, just as long as they accomplish a goal which matters to them.

Preferences

Animators cannot bear routine and repetitiveness. When they have to carry out a monotonous and repetitious task, they will try to lend variety and attraction to the job by introducing elements of variety and diversity to it. A great many of them, intent on avoiding a lifetime spent at a desk or under the eagle eye of the boss, will consciously choose work which takes them out and about, demanding travel and meetings with contractors and clients, but providing a greater degree of freedom. Their innate activeness, enterprise, liking for risk and thirst for independence mean that many *animators* set up their own companies and become successful in the business world.

Skills and stumbling blocks

As a rule, *animators* do better at tasks requiring spontaneity and fast reactions rather than good planning, sensible organisation and methodical execution. As a result, when they hold supervisory or managerial positions, they need the strong support of assistants or secretaries to whom they can assign all their practical, routine duties. Problems where emotions and feelings play a large part are also a stumbling block. Since they feel on very uncertain ground when they enter areas demanding intuition and empathy and requiring them to read human emotions, they will do everything they can to avoid situations of that kind.

As part of a team

To *animators*, a good boss is a boss who sets out the general course of action for their subordinates and then leaves them alone to get on with the job. They are happy to work as part of a group, contributing optimism, enthusiasm and a practical approach to problems. They are natural inspirers and initiators and will often be the first to get to work, spurring others to follow suit. Their fervour, enthusiasm and engagement are a positive inspiration and motivating force. They themselves will most happily work with people whose openness and spontaneity is similar to their own and who are gifted with a sense of humour and the ability to enjoy life.

Animators suffer when they have to cooperate with people who are incapable of taking responsibility for their own lives or who see the world in gloomy hues. They fail to comprehend those who manage to spend months chewing over a problem without taking so much as a single practical step aimed at solving it. To *animators*, theoretical debate is not only stupendously tiresome, but is also unproductive, signifying a waste of time and energy. In turn, their own actions can be perceived as hasty, ill-conceived, premature and chaotic.

Professions

Knowledge of our own personality profile and natural preferences provides us with invaluable help in choosing the optimal path in our professional careers. Experience has shown that, while *animators* are perfectly able to work and find fulfilment in a range of fields, their personality type naturally predisposes them to the following fields and professions:

- acting
- animateur
- anti-terrorism
- bodyguard
- the construction industry
- crisis management
- driver

- electrician
- electronics
- engineer
- entrepreneur
- estate agent
- financial advisor
- firefighter
- insurance agent
- lifeguard
- locksmith
- logistics
- metalworker
- photographer
- physiotherapist
- police officer
- radio presenter
- sales assistant
- sales representative
- security guard
- soldier
- sportswoman/sportsman
- television presenter
- tour guide
- tourist/holiday resort representative
- sports coach
- travel agent

Potential strengths and weaknesses

Like any other personality type, *animators* have their potential strengths and weaknesses and this potential can be cultivated in a variety of ways. *Animators'* personal happiness and professional fulfilment depend on whether they make the most of the 'pluses' offered by their personality type and face up to its inherent dangers. Here, then, is a SUMMARY of those 'pluses' and dangers:

Potential strengths

Animators are open, optimistic and quick to establish contact with others. They hold no grudges, but are able to forgive both other people and themselves. They live for today, enjoying the here and now and not tormenting themselves with thoughts of past mistakes. Splendid observers, with excellent memories, they are characterised by their uncommon flexibility and spontaneity, find change easy to handle and adapt rapidly to new circumstances. Being unusually logical and rational, they enjoy tackling practical problems and have no fear of 'insoluble' tasks. They have the ability to size up a situation rapidly and, with their extraordinary gift for improvisation, to respond appropriately to problems and changing circumstances as they crop up. Efficient, enterprising and energetic, they cope well in situations of conflict, are impervious to criticism and, when convinced that they should take a particular action, they are capable of doing so regardless of the views and opinions of others. Dissuading them is something of a challenge.

By nature bold and unafraid of risk, *animators* infect others with their enthusiasm and faith that their undertakings will succeed. They initiate all kinds of activities and motivate others to work.

Capable of investing their entire energy in a task that matters to them, they are just as good at relaxing. As a rule, they are superb oral communicators, keeping their listeners riveted with their colourful, witty and fascinating way with the spoken word. They also possess the gift of persuasiveness.

Potential weaknesses

Animators have a problem with defining priorities and with operating methodically and systematically, being prone to act impulsively. Their activities are usually reactions to immediate problems and challenges; they will rarely be the result of planned actions taken with the future in mind. Focused as they are on the here and now, they have trouble identifying future opportunities and threats, as well as with foreseeing the consequences of their actions and their impact on other people. They are easily distracted. When they catch sight of a new challenge, their enthusiasm for things they have already started doing dissolves and, as a result, they have problems with keeping their promises and seeing things through to the end. Their poor planning and time management skills can sometimes mean that they fail to organise their tasks properly, missing deadlines as a consequence.

Animators cope badly with tasks requiring them to work alone and demanding lengthy preparation by way of reading large amounts of material, for instance, or drawing up a detailed plan of action. In general, they do no better when it comes to routine tasks and repetitive activities and anything which entails abstract thinking or looking ahead to the future will also be a problem for them. By nature impatient and quick to tire of situations, they are also frequently characterised by an inclination towards risk and dicing with danger. Their self-assurance usually helps them to succeed; however, on occasion, it can lead them to overestimate their capabilities or underrate the seriousness of a problem. Despite their excellent interpersonal relationships in the social sphere, *animators* have difficulty both in reading the emotions and feelings of others and in expressing their own. It can happen that they hurt other people with their explicit or critical remarks, while they themselves remain completely unaware of the impact of their words.

Personal development

Animators' personal development depends on the extent to which they make use of their natural potential and surmount the dangers inherent in their personality type. What follows are some practical tips which, together, form a specific guide that we might call *The Animator's Ten Commandments*.

Admit that you can make mistakes

Things may be more complex than they seem to you. You may not always be in the right. Bring that thought to the forefront of your mind before you start accusing others or pointing out their mistakes and reproaching them.

Learn to set priorities and manage your time

Enthusiasm is your main driving force. Nonetheless, listing priorities, establishing time frames and planning out a job are not at all the same thing as forging chains to shackle your creativity, fetter your activities and encumber you as you carry out the task. Perish the thought! They are tools and when you use them properly, they will help you achieve the goals you are aiming for.

Praise others

Make the most of every occasion to appreciate other people, say something nice to them and praise them for something they have done. At work, value people not only for the job they do, but also for who they are. Then wait and see. The difference will come as a pleasant surprise!

Be more understanding

Show others more warmth. Remember that not everyone should be assigned the same tasks, because not everyone is skilled in the same fields. If someone is unable to cope with a task, this is not always a sign of their ill will or laziness.

Appreciate the worth of creative ideas

Operating solely on the basis of dry facts and hard data brings a whole range of restrictions in its wake. Many a problem can only be solved by intuition, an innovative approach and thinking creatively. So stay open to them all!

Give some thought to the future

With most of your attention focused on current tasks and immediate goals, you might well be overlooking future opportunities. Why miss out? To make the most of them, all you need do is give some thought to what you want to achieve over the next year, the next five years and the next decade.

Keep your impulsiveness reigned in

Before you make a decision or commit yourself to a venture, devote a little time to gathering some relevant information and analysing it. When you take that approach, you will most likely find yourself with less to do and, more to the point, you will end up doing it better.

Criticise less

Not everyone has your ability to handle constructive criticism. In many cases, it can have a destructive effect. Studies have shown that praising positive behaviour, albeit limited, motivates people more than criticising negative conduct. When you comment on the behaviour and viewpoints of others, exercise more restraint.

Finish what you start

You launch into new things enthusiastically but have problems with finishing what you have already started, a *modus operandi* which usually produces mediocre results. Try sorting out what is most important to you and deciding how you want to accomplish it. Then knuckle down and turn your back firmly on all those tempting distractions!

Remember important dates and anniversaries

Arrangements to meet people, the birthdays of those closest to you and family anniversaries may seem like rather trivial matters to you in comparison to whatever it is you are involved in. They matter a great deal to other people, though. So if you are incapable of remembering them, jot them down somewhere handy ... and then remember to check those notes!

Well-known figures

Below is a list of some well-known people who match the *animator's* profile:

- **Sir Winston Churchill** (1874-1965); a British politician, orator, strategist, author and historian. He served twice as prime minister of the United Kingdom and wrote numerous outstanding historical works, winning the Nobel Prize for Literature.
- **Ernest Hemingway** (1899-1961); an American author whose works include *The Old Man and the Sea*, he was awarded the Nobel Prize for Literature.
- **Evita** (María Eva Duarte de Perón; 1919-1952); an Argentinean screen and radio actress also famed as a political and social activist.

- **Mikhail Kalashnikov** (1919-2013); a Russian weapons designer and the creator of the AK-47 automatic assault rifle, widely known as the 'Kalashnikov'.
- **Peter Falk** (1927-2011); an American screen actor whose filmography includes the title role in the *Columbo* TV series.
- **Jack Nicholson** (born in 1937); an American screen actor whose films include *One Flew Over the Cuckoo's Nest*, he is also a director, screenwriter and producer and the holder of numerous prestigious awards.
- **John Rhys-Davies** (born in 1944); a Welsh screen and voice actor whose films include *The Lord of the Rings*.
- **Madonna** (Madonna Louise Veronica Ciccone; born in 1958); an American singer, songwriter and actress of Italian and French-Canadian descent, she has won numerous prestigious awards.
- **Antonio Banderas** (José Antonio Domínguez Bandera; born in 1960); a Spanish screen actor whose films include *Desperado*, he is also a director and producer and the winner of numerous prestigious awards.
- **Jeremy Clarkson** (born in 1960); an English print and media journalist and television presenter whose TV shows include *Top Gear*.

- **Michal J. Fox** (born in 1961); a Canadian-American film actor, author and producer whose films include *Back to the Future*.

- **Mike Tyson** (Michael Gerard Tyson; born in 1966); an American boxer and former world heavyweight champion, now retired from the ring.

- **Matt Damon** (born in 1970); an American film actor whose films include *Good Will Hunting*, he is also a screenwriter and producer.

- **David Tennant** (David MacDonald; born in 1971); a British stage, screen and voice actor whose filmography includes the title role in the *Doctor Who* TV series.

- **Britney Spears** (born in 1981); an American pop singer, dancer and screen actress.

The ID16™© Personality Types in a Nutshell

The Administrator (ESTJ)

Life motto: We'll get the job done!

Administrators are hard-working, responsible and extremely loyal. Energetic and decisive, they value order, stability, security and clear rules. They are matter-of-fact and businesslike, logical, rational and practical and possess the capability to assimilate large amounts of detailed information.

Superb organisers, they are intolerant of ineffectuality, wastefulness and slothfulness. True to their convictions and direct in their contact with others, they present their point of view decisively and openly express critical opinions, sometimes hurting other people as a result.

The *administrator's* four natural inclinations:

- source of life energy: the exterior world
- mode of assimilating information: via the senses
- decision-making mode: the mind
- lifestyle: organised

Similar personality types:

- the Animator
- the Inspector
- the Practitioner

Statistical data:

- *administrators* constitute between ten and thirteen per cent of the global community
- men predominate among *administrators* (60 per cent)
- the United States is an example of a nation corresponding to the *administrator's* profile [3]

Find out more!

The Administrator. Your Guide to the ESTJ Personality Type by Jaroslaw Jankowski

---

[3] What this means is not that all the residents of the USA fall within this personality type, but that American society as a whole possesses a great many of the character traits typical of the *administrator*.

The Advocate (ESFJ)

Life motto: How can I help you?

Advocates are well-organised, energetic and enthusiastic. Practical, responsible and conscientious, they are sincere and exceptionally gregarious.

Advocates are perceptive of human feelings, emotions and needs. They value harmony and find criticism and conflict difficult to bear. With their sensitivity to any and every manifestation of injustice, prejudice or detriment to another, they are genuinely interested in other people's problems and take real delight in helping them and tending to their needs, while often neglecting their own. They have a tendency to do everything for others and can be vulnerable to manipulation.

The *advocate*'s four natural inclinations:

- source of life energy: the exterior world
- mode of assimilating information: via the senses
- decision-making mode: the heart
- lifestyle: organised

Similar personality types:

- the Presenter
- the Protector
- the Artist

Statistical data:

- *advocates* constitute between ten and thirteen per cent of the global community
- women predominate among *advocates* (70 per cent)
- Canada is an example of a nation corresponding to the *advocate's* profile

Find out more!

The Advocate. Your Guide to the ESFJ Personality Type by Jaroslaw Jankowski

The Animator (ESTP)

Life motto: Let's DO something!

Animators are energetic, active and enterprising. Fond of the company of others, they have the ability to enjoy the moment and are spontaneous, flexible and open to change.

Animators are inspirers and instigators, spurring others to act. Being logical, rational and pragmatic realists, they are wearied by abstract concepts and solutions for the future. Their focus is on solving concrete problems in the here and now. They have difficulties with organising and planning and can be impulsive, acting first and thinking later.

The *animator's* four natural inclinations:

- source of life energy: the exterior world
- mode of assimilating information: via the senses

- decision-making mode: the mind
- lifestyle: spontaneous

Similar personality types:

- the Administrator
- the Practitioner
- the Inspector

Statistical data:

- *animators* constitute between six and ten per cent of the global community
- men predominate among *animators* (60 per cent)
- Australia is an example of a nation corresponding to the *animator's* profile

Find out more!

The Animator. Your Guide to the ESTP Personality Type by Jaroslaw Jankowski

The Artist (ISFP)

Life motto: Let's create something!

Artists are sensitive, creative and original, with a sense of the aesthetic and natural artistic talents. Independent in character, they follow their own system of values and are optimistic in outlook, with a positive approach to life and an ability to enjoy the moment.

Helping others is a source of joy to them. They find abstract theories tedious and would rather create reality than talk about it, although starting on something new comes more easily to them than finishing what they have already started. They have difficulty in voicing their own desires and needs.

The *artist's* four natural inclinations:

- source of life energy: the interior world
- mode of assimilating information: via the senses
- decision-making mode: the heart
- lifestyle: spontaneous

Similar personality types:

- the Protector
- the Presenter
- the Advocate

Statistical data:

- *artists* constitute between six and nine per cent of the global community
- women predominate among *artists* (60 per cent)
- China is an example of a nation corresponding to the *artist's* profile

Find out more!

The Artist. Your Guide to the ISFP Personality Type by Jaroslaw Jankowski

The Counsellor (ENFJ)

Life motto: My friends are my world

Counsellors are optimistic, enthusiastic and quick-witted. Courteous and tactful, they have an extraordinary gift for empathy and find joy in acting for the good of others, with no thought of themselves. They have the ability to influence other people, inspiring them, eliciting their hidden potential and giving them faith in their own powers. Radiating warmth, they draw others to them and often help them in solving their personal problems.

Counsellors can be over-trusting and have a tendency to view the world through rose-tinted glasses. With their focus on other people, they often forget about their own needs.

The *counsellor's* four natural inclinations:

- source of life energy: the exterior world
- mode of assimilating information: intuition
- decision-making mode: the heart
- lifestyle: organised

Similar personality types:

- the Enthusiast
- the Mentor
- the Idealist

Statistical data:

- *counsellors* constitute between three and five per cent of the global community
- women predominate among *counsellors* (80 per cent)
- France is an example of a nation corresponding to the *counsellor's* profile

Find out more!

The Counsellor. Your Guide to the ENFJ Personality Type by Jaroslaw Jankowski

The Director (ENTJ)

Life motto: I'll tell you what you need to do.

Directors are independent, active and decisive. Rational, logical and creative, when they analyse problems they look at the wider picture and are able to foresee the future consequences of human activities. They are characterised by optimism and a healthy sense of their own worth and are capable of transforming theoretical concepts into concrete, practical plans of action.

Visionaries, mentors and organisers, *directors* possess natural leadership skills. Their powerful personalities and direct and critical style can often have an intimidating effect, causing them problems in their interpersonal relationships.

The *director's* four natural inclinations:

- source of life energy: the exterior world

- mode of assimilating information: intuition
- decision-making mode: the mind
- lifestyle: organised

Similar personality types:

- the Innovator
- the Strategist
- the Logician

Statistical data:

- *directors* constitute between two and five per cent of the global community
- men predominate among *directors* (70 per cent)
- Holland is an example of a nation corresponding to the *director's* profile

Find out more!

The Director. Your Guide to the ENTJ Personality Type by Jaroslaw Jankowski

The Enthusiast (ENFP)

Life motto: We'll manage!

Enthusiasts are energetic, enthusiastic and optimistic. Capable of enjoying life and looking ahead to the future, they are dynamic, quick-witted and creative. They have a liking for people in general, value honest and genuine relationships and are warm, sincere and emotional. Criticism is something they handle badly. With their gift for empathy and ability to perceive people's needs, feelings and motives, they both inspire others and infect them with their own enthusiasm.

They love to be at the centre of events and are flexible and capable of improvising. Their inclination leads towards idealistic notions. Being easily distracted, they have problems with seeing things through to the end.

The *enthusiast's* four natural inclinations:

- source of life energy: the exterior world
- mode of assimilating information: intuition
- decision-making mode: the heart
- lifestyle: spontaneous

Similar personality types:

- the Counsellor
- the Idealist
- the Mentor

Statistical data:

- *enthusiasts* constitute between five and eight per cent of the global community
- women predominate among *enthusiasts* (60 per cent)
- Italy is an example of a nation corresponding to the *enthusiast's* profile

Find out more!

The Enthusiast. Your Guide to the ENFP Personality Type by Jaroslaw Jankowski

The Idealist (INFP)

Life motto: We CAN live differently.

Idealists are sensitive, loyal, and creative. Living in accordance with the values they hold is of immense importance to them and they both manifest an interest in the reality of the spirit and delve deeply into the mysteries of life. Wrapped up in the world's problems and open to the needs of other people, they prize harmony and balance.

Idealists are romantic; not only are they able to show love, but they also need warmth and affection themselves. With their outstanding ability to read other people's feelings and emotions, they build healthy, profound and enduring relationships. They feel that they are on very shaky ground in situations of conflict and have no real resistance to stress and criticism.

The *idealist's* four natural inclinations:

- source of life energy: the interior world
- mode of assimilating information: intuition
- decision-making mode: the heart
- lifestyle: spontaneous

Similar personality types:

- the Mentor
- the Enthusiast
- the Counsellor

Statistical data:

- *idealists* constitute between one and four per cent of the global community
- women predominate among *idealists* (60 per cent)
- Thailand is an example of a nation corresponding to the *idealist's* profile

Find out more!

The Idealist. Your Guide to the INFP Personality Type by Jaroslaw Jankowski

The Innovator (ENTP)

Life motto: How about trying a different approach…?

Innovators are inventive, original and independent. Optimistic, energetic and enterprising, they are people of action who love being at the centre of events and solving 'insoluble' problems. Their thoughts are turned to the future and they are curious about the world and visionary by nature. Open to new concepts and ideas, they enjoy new experiences and experiments and have the ability to identify the connections between separate events.

Innovators are spontaneous, communicative and self-assured. However, they tend to overestimate their own possibilities and have problems with seeing things through to the end. They are also inclined to be impatient and to take risks.

The *innovator's* four natural inclinations:

- source of life energy: the exterior world
- mode of assimilating information: intuition
- decision-making mode: the mind
- lifestyle: spontaneous

Similar personality types:

- the Director
- the Logician
- the Strategist

Statistical data:

- *innovators* constitute between three and five per cent of the global community
- men predominate among *innovators* (70 per cent)
- Israel is an example of a nation corresponding to the *innovator's* profile

Find out more!

The Innovator. Your Guide to the ENTP Personality Type by Jaroslaw Jankowski

The Inspector (ISTJ)

Life motto: *Duty first.*

Inspectors are people who can always be counted on. Well-mannered, punctual, reliable, conscientious and responsible, when they give their word, they keep it. Being analytical, methodical, systematic and logical by nature, they tend be seen as serious, cold and reserved. They prize calm, stability and order, have no fondness for change and like clear principles and concrete rules.

Inspectors are hard-working, persevering and capable of seeing things through to the end. As perfectionists, they try to exercise control over everything within their sphere and are sparing in their praise. They also underrate the importance of other people's feelings and emotions.

The *inspector's* four natural inclinations:

- source of life energy: the interior world
- mode of assimilating information: via the senses
- decision-making mode: the mind
- lifestyle: organised

Similar personality types:

- the Practitioner
- the Administrator
- the Animator

Statistical data:

- *inspectors* constitute between six and ten per cent of the global community
- men predominate among *inspectors* (60 per cent)
- Switzerland is an example of a nation corresponding to the *inspector's* profile

Find out more!

The Inspector. Your Guide to the ISTJ Personality Type by Jaroslaw Jankowski

The Logician (INTP)

Life motto: Above all else, seek to discover the truths about the world.

Logicians are original, resourceful and creative. With a love for solving problems of a theoretical nature, they are analytical, quick-witted, enthusiastically disposed towards new concepts and have the ability to connect individual phenomena, educing general rules and theories from them. Logical, exact and inquiring, they are quick to spot incoherence and inconsistency.

Logicians are independent, sceptical of existing solutions and authorities, tolerant and open to new challenges. When immersed in thought, they will sometimes lose touch with the outside world.

The *logician's* four natural inclinations:

- source of life energy: the interior world

- mode of assimilating information: intuition
- decision-making mode: the mind
- lifestyle: spontaneous

Similar personality types:

- the Strategist
- the Innovator
- the Director

Statistical data:

- *logicians* constitute between two and three per cent of the global community;
- men predominate among *logicians* (80 per cent)
- India is an example of a nation corresponding to the *logician's* profile

Find out more!

The Logician. Your Guide to the INTP Personality Type by Jaroslaw Jankowski

The Mentor (INFJ)

Life motto: The world CAN be a better place!

Mentors are creative and sensitive. With their gaze fixed firmly on the future, they spot opportunities and potential imperceptible to others. Idealists and visionaries, they are geared towards helping people and are conscientious, responsible and, at one and the same time, courteous, caring and friendly. They strive to understand the mechanisms governing the world and view problems from a wide perspective.

Superb listeners and observers, *mentors* are characterised by their extraordinary empathy, intuition and trust of people and are capable of reading the feelings and emotions of others. They find criticism and conflict difficult to bear and can come across as enigmatic.

The *mentor's* four natural inclinations:

- source of life energy: the interior world
- mode of assimilating information: intuition
- decision-making mode: the heart
- lifestyle: organised

Similar personality types:

- the Idealist
- the Counsellor
- the Enthusiast

Statistical data:

- *mentors* constitute one per cent of the global community and are the most rarely occurring of the sixteen personality types
- women predominate among *mentors* (80 per cent)
- Norway is an example of a nation corresponding to the *mentor's* profile

Find out more!

The Mentor. Your Guide to the INFJ Personality Type by Jaroslaw Jankowski

The Practitioner (ISTP)

Life motto: Actions speak louder than words.

Practitioners are optimistic and spontaneous, with a positive approach to life. Reserved and independent, they hold true to their personal convictions and view external principles and norms with scepticism. They find abstract concepts and solutions for the future tiresome and would far rather roll up their sleeves and get to work on solving tangible and concrete problems.

Adapting well to new places and situations, they enjoy fresh challenges and risks and are capable of keeping a cool head in the face of threats and danger. Their general reticence and extreme reserve when it comes to expressing their opinions mean that other people may often find them impenetrable.

The *practitioner's* four natural inclinations:

- source of life energy: the interior world
- mode of assimilating information: via the senses
- decision-making mode: the mind
- lifestyle: spontaneous

Similar personality types:

- the Inspector
- the Animator
- the Administrator

Statistical data:

- *practitioners* constitute between six and nine per cent of the global community
- men predominate among *practitioners* (60 per cent)
- Singapore is an example of a nation corresponding to the *practitioner's* profile

Find out more!

The Practitioner. Your Guide to the ISTP Personality Type by Jaroslaw Jankowski

The Presenter (ESFP)

Life motto: Now is the perfect moment!

Presenters are optimistic, energetic and outgoing, with the ability to enjoy life and have fun to the full. Practical, flexible and spontaneous at one and the same time, they enjoy change and new experiences, coping badly with solitude, stagnation and routine.

With their liking for being at the centre of attention, they are natural-born actors and their speaking abilities arouse the interest and enthusiasm of their listeners. Focused as they are on the present moment, they will sometimes lose sight of their long-term aims and can also have problems with foreseeing the consequences of their actions.

The *presenter's* four natural inclinations:

- source of life energy: the exterior world
- mode of assimilating information: via the senses
- decision-making mode: the heart
- lifestyle: spontaneous

Similar personality types:

- the Advocate
- the Artist
- the Protector

Statistical data:

- *presenters* constitute between eight and thirteen per cent of the global community
- women predominate among *presenters* (60 per cent)
- Brazil is an example of a nation corresponding to the *presenter's* profile

Find out more!

The Presenter. Your Guide to the ESFP Personality Type by Jaroslaw Jankowski

The Protector (ISFJ)

Life motto: Your happiness matters to me.

Protectors are sincere, warm-hearted, unassuming, trustworthy and extraordinarily loyal. With their ability to perceive people's needs and their desire to help them, they will always put others first. Practical, well-organised and gifted with both an eye and a memory for detail, they are responsible, hard-working, patient, persevering and capable of seeing things through to the end.

Protectors set great store by tranquillity, stability and friendly relations with others and are skilled at building bridges between people. By the same token, they find conflict and criticism difficult to bear. Given their powerful sense of duty and their constant readiness to come to the aid of others, they can end up being used by people.

The *protector's* four natural inclinations:

- source of life energy: the interior world
- mode of assimilating information: via the senses
- decision-making mode: the heart
- lifestyle: organised

Similar personality types:

- the Artist
- the Advocate
- the Presenter

Statistical data:

- *protectors* constitute between eight and twelve per cent of the global population
- women predominate among *protectors* (70 per cent)
- Sweden is an example of a nation corresponding to the *protector's* profile

Find out more!

The Protector. Your Guide to the ISFJ Personality Type by Jaroslaw Jankowski

The Strategist (INTJ)

Life motto: I can certainly improve this.

Strategists are independent and outstandingly individualistic, with an immense seam of inner energy. Creative, inventive and resourceful, others perceive them as competent, self-assured and, at one and the same time, distant and enigmatic. No matter what they turn their attention to, they will always look at the bigger picture and they have a driving urge to improve the world around them and set it in order.

Well-organised, responsible, critical and demanding, they are difficult to knock off balance – and just as hard to please to the full. Reading the emotions and feelings of others is something they find very problematic.

The *strategist's* four natural inclinations:

- source of life energy: the interior world
- mode of assimilating information: intuition
- decision-making mode: the mind
- lifestyle: organised

Similar personality types:

- the Logician
- the Director
- the Innovator

Statistical data:

- *strategists* constitute between one and two per cent of the global community
- men predominate among *strategists* (80 per cent)
- Finland is an example of a nation corresponding to the *strategist's* profile

Find out more!

The Strategist. Your Guide to the INTJ Personality Type by Jaroslaw Jankowski

Additional information

The four natural inclinations

1. THE DOMINANT SOURCE OF LIFE ENERGY

   a. THE EXTERIOR WORLD
      People who draw their energy from outside. They need activity and contact with others and find being alone for any length of time hard to bear.

   b. THE INTERIOR WORLD
      People who draw their energy from their inner world. They need quiet and solitude and feel drained

when they spend any length of time in a group.

2. THE DOMINANT MODE OF ASSIMILATING INFORMATION

    a. VIA THE SENSES
       People who rely on the five senses and are persuaded by facts and evidence. They have a liking for methods and practices which are tried and tested and prefer concrete tasks and are realists who trust in experience.

    b. VIA INTUITION
       People who rely on the sixth sense and are driven by what they 'feel in their bones'. They have a liking for innovative solutions and problems of a theoretical nature and are characterised by a creative approach to their tasks and the ability to predict.

3. THE DOMINANT DECISION-MAKING MODE

    a. THE MIND
       People who are guided by logic and objective principles. They are critical and direct in expressing their opinions.

b. THE HEART
People who are guided by their feelings and values. They long for harmony and mutual understanding with others.

4. THE DOMINANT LIFESTYLE

a. ORGANISED
People who are conscientious and organised. They value order and like to operate according to plan.

b. SPONTANEOUS
People who are spontaneous and value freedom of action. They live for the moment and have no trouble finding their feet in new situations.

The approximate percentage of each personality type in the world population

Personality Type:	Proportion:
• The Administrator (ESTJ):	10-13%
• The Advocate (ESFJ):	10-13%
• The Animator (ESTP):	6-10%
• The Artist (ISFP):	6-9%
• The Counsellor (ENFJ):	3-5 %
• The Director (ENTJ):	2-5%
• The Enthusiast (ENFP):	5-8%

- The Idealist (INFP):   1-4%
- The Innovator (ENTP):   3-5%
- The Inspector (ISTJ):   6-10%
- The Logician (INTP):   2-3%
- The Mentor (INFJ):   ca. 1%
- The Practitioner (ISTP):   6-9%
- The Presenter (ESFP):   8-13%
- The Protector (ISFJ):   8-12%
- The Strategist (INTJ):   1-2%

The approximate percentage of women and men of each personality type in the world population

Personality Type:	Women / Men:
The Administrator (ESTJ):	40% / 60%
The Advocate (ESFJ):	70% / 30%
The Animator (ESTP):	40% / 60%
The Artist (ISFP):	60% / 40%
The Counsellor (ENFJ):	80% / 20%
The Director (ENTJ):	30% / 70%
The Enthusiast (ENFP):	60% / 40%
The Idealist (INFP):	60% / 40%
The Innovator (ENTP):	30% / 70%
The Inspector (ISTJ):	40% / 60%
The Logician (INTP):	20% / 80%
The Mentor (INFJ):	80% / 20%
The Practitioner (ISTP):	40% / 60%
The Presenter (ESFP):	60% / 40%
The Protector (ISFJ):	70% / 30%
The Strategist (INTJ):	20% / 80%

Bibliography

- Arraj, Tyra & Arraj, James: *Tracking the Elusive Human, Volume 1: A Practical Guide to C.G. Jung's Psychological Types, W.H. Sheldon's Body and Temperament Types and Their Integration*, Inner Growth Books, 1988
- Arraj, James: *Tracking the Elusive Human, Volume 2: An Advanced Guide to the Typological Worlds of C. G. Jung, W.H. Sheldon, Their Integration, and the Biochemical Typology of the Future*, Inner Growth Books, 1990
- Berens, Linda V.; Cooper, Sue A.; Ernst, Linda K.; Martin, Charles R.; Myers, Steve; Nardi, Dario; Pearman, Roger R.; Segal, Marci; Smith, Melissa: *A Quick Guide to the 16 Personality Types in Organizations: Understanding Personality Differences in the Workplace*, Telos Publications, 2002

- Geier, John G. & Downey, E. Dorothy: *Energetics of Personality*, Aristos Publishing House, 1989
- Hunsaker, Phillip L. & Alessandra, Anthony J.: *The Art of Managing People*, Simon and Schuster, 1986
- Jung, Carl Gustav: *Psychological Types (The Collected Works of C. G. Jung, Vol. 6)*, Princeton University Press, 1976
- Kise, Jane A. G.; Stark, David & Krebs Hirsch, Sandra: *LifeKeys: Discover Who You Are*, Bethany House, 2005
- Kroeger, Otto & Thuesen, Janet: *Type Talk or How to Determine Your Personality Type and Change Your Life*, Delacorte Press, 1988
- Lawrence, Gordon: *People Types and Tiger Stripes*, Center for Applications of Psychological Type, 1993
- Lawrence, Gordon: *Looking at Type and Learning Styles*, Center for Applications of Psychological Type, 1997
- Maddi, Salvatore R.: *Personality Theories: A Comparative Analysis*, Waveland, 2001
- Martin, Charles R.: *Looking at Type: The Fundamentals Using Psychological Type To Understand and Appreciate Ourselves and Others*, Center for Applications of Psychological Type, 2001
- Meier C.A.: Personality: *The Individuation Process in the Light of C. G. Jung's Typology*, Daimon Verlag, 2007

- Pearman, Roger R. & Albritton, Sarah: *I'm Not Crazy, I'm Just Not You: The Real Meaning of the Sixteen Personality Types*, Davies-Black Publishing, 1997

- Segal, Marci: Creativity and Personality Type: *Tools for Understanding and Inspiring the Many Voices of Creativity*, Telos Publications, 2001

- Sharp, Daryl: Personality Type: *Jung's Model of Typology*, Inner City Books, 1987

- Spoto, Angelo: *Jung's Typology in Perspective*, Chiron Publications, 1995

- Tannen, Deborah: *You Just Don't Understand*, William Morrow and Company, 1990

- Thomas, Jay C. & Segal, Daniel L.: *Comprehensive Handbook of Personality and Psychopathology, Personality and Everyday Functioning*, Wiley, 2005

- Thomson, Lenore: *Personality Type: An Owner's Manual*, Shambhala, 1998

- Tieger, Paul D. & Barron-Tieger Barbara: *Just Your Type: Create the Relationship You've Always Wanted Using the Secrets of Personality Type*, Little, Brown and Company, 2000

- Von Franz, Marie-Louise & Hillman, James: *Lectures on Jung's Typology*, Continuum International Publishing Group, 1971

www.ingramcontent.com/pod-product-compliance
Lightning Source LLC
Chambersburg PA
CBHW031208020426
42333CB00013B/845